H O M E S I C K

Bart Millard of MercyMe

Homesick

"Make two homes for thyself...one actual home...

and another spiritual home,

which thou art to carry with thee always."

- ST. CATHERINE OF SIENA

We are all homesick. I think it goes back to the moment Adam and Eve took that first bite. The sweet taste of fruit was still on their lips when they felt an unfamiliar ache. A longing for something — for someone — for somewhere else. They were homesick.

For Earth's first couple, freshly banished from paradise, this separation was a new sensation. For us, it's an ever-present awareness. I have felt its tug more at some times than at others—my first day of school, leaving home, welcoming my children into the world and thinking about the day when I will have to let them go, watching family and loved ones slip away — but the feeling that something's missing will never fully go away this side of Heaven.

And that's probably as it should be. After all, this world is not our home.

WE'RE ALL HOMESICK.

5

"There's no place like home."

- DOROTHY GALE IN THE WIZARD OF OZ

What is this place called home? Is it where I hang my heart or where I lay my head? Maybe it's a little of both. Home for me is wherever my wife, Shannon, and our two kids are. But it's also a place for me. Those four walls represent an emotional sigh of relief because once inside, I can let my hair down. I can be myself — blemishes and all — and I'm loved just the same. I just feel better in my skin when I'm home.

I've read somewhere that more than seven million people in the US buy homes each month. I see countless home-improvement TV shows, huge do-it-yourself stores, and rows of books on the subject of home. It is apparent that this whole idea of "home" has a strong hold on us, and there is something ingrained in our nature that makes us want to find comfort and settle down in one place.

This world may not be our final destination, but that doesn't stop us from trying to make ourselves at home here. We settle in, take on a mortgage, hang up pictures, and tend our yard. But no matter how hard we try to establish deep roots, we're not meant to stay.

When I'm on the road, I miss the predictability and consistency of everyday life back home. Sleeping in my own bed, my own place on the mattress. Getting up early to fix my son Sam's breakfast while I catch the latest sports headlines on TV. It's such a powerful connection between my heart and home that even when I'm on the road, I'll find myself waking up at 7 a.m. My family is hundreds of miles away so there are no kids for me to feed, but in the fog of early morning, my heart sometimes forgets.

Don't get me wrong, I wouldn't trade what I do for anything — I think you can love your job so much that you actually feel guilty about doing it — but nothing compares to home. Nothing.

"I close my eyes and I see your face.

If home is where the heart is, then I'm out of place."

- FROM THE MERCYME SONG "HOMESICK"

photo by Charles Brock

It's a rite of passage, that first night spent away from home. I'll never forget my first time. To some, it can be exciting, but it can also be terrifying. Away from everything that signifies security, the world can seem pretty scary. It's the point at which most of us are first introduced to that powerful emotion known as homesickness.

GREENVILLE
CITY LIMIT
POP. 23071

18

photo by Jim Bryson

Greenville, Texas is also home. Population 23,000 and some change. I grew up in this town — the town that in some ways raised me. My wife's parents were my first-grade Sunday school teachers. People went the extra mile to show me right from wrong, and there are families all over town that had a hand in making me the man I am today. The town of Greenville and the people who live here are home to me. No matter where I go in this world, there's always something that reminds me of home.

"Home is where one starts."

-T. S. ELIOT

photo by Jim Bryson

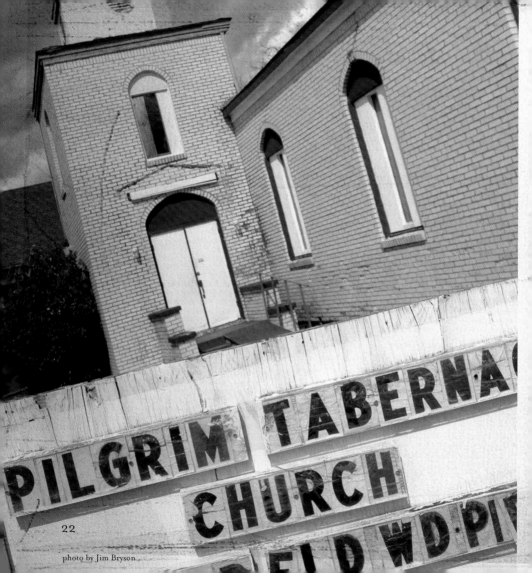

PILGRIM TABERNAC
CHURCH
EID WD PI

22

What makes a place a home? A little bit of everything. It's security, it's belonging, it's not needing a road map, it's knowing everyone's names. Away from home and in the whirlwind of life, so many people are just competing with each other and striving for more and more. But at home, folks root for each other. You don't have to impress them. Get thirteenth place in something, and they'd still be proud.

Home is like this sweet, elderly lady at my church who tells everyone they sing great because she doesn't want to hurt their feelings. Home is a place that cares, and it's where we get filled up so we can face another day.

"Absence makes the heart grow fonder."

-SEXTUS PROPERTIUS
ROMAN POET

45

My dad died when I was 19, and my grandmother had moved in a year earlier to help take care of us while he was sick. When the time came for me to leave home, I said good-bye to my grandmother, got into the car, and then it struck me — her son is gone, and now I'm leaving her. A mile down the road, I started crying and I couldn't stop. I didn't know how I could possibly go through with it. Fortunately, there were two friends with me who refused to let me turn around.

What teenager hasn't thought, "If I can just get out of this place — I've got big plans." Many of them do eventually pack their bags and strike out on their own. I was one of them. But when the moment of truth arrived, I was torn.

Everyone has to venture out at some point, to discover for themselves just where they belong. I had my questions about leaving, but something inside of me kept pushing me forward.

photo by Jim Bryson

When I lived in Florida, Oklahoma, and Tennessee, I still felt like a kid away from home. It was always about going back to Texas on break. I realize that just because you get mail at a certain location, doesn't automatically make it home.

"Lord, won't you give me the strength to make it through somehow? I've never been more homesick than now."

- FROM THE SONG "HOMESICK"

"It's when you're safe at home that you wish you were having an adventure. When you're having an adventure, you wish you were safe at home."

- THORNTON WILDER

I like the story of the prodigal son. He's usually seen as rebellious and worldly — the proverbial "bad seed"— but there's a little of him inside all of us. I, too, needed to break away to some degree. Of course, his wild lifestyle could have been the end of him and it nearly was. His father was certainly under no obligation to take him back. Fortunately, the story had a happy ending. But it was really just the beginning. I can't help but wonder what happened next. How did his experiences — and his homesickness — change the life he went on to live?

"...While we are at home in the body,

we are absent from the Lord."

- 2 CORINTHIANS 5:6B

I think if you live long enough, you reach a point where you have more invested in Heaven than here on Earth. In other words, you have more loved ones in Heaven than there are people you love still here on Earth with you. That was something I hoped I wouldn't feel until I was 60, 65, maybe 70 years old. But after losing way too many people who were close to me, I feel it now at 32.

DIED
Dec. 17, 19__

IN MEMORY OF
WOODMEN OF THE
WORLD MEM.
GROVE

I know home is supposed to be where the heart is, but sometimes my

heart feels like it's split in two between Earth and Heaven. I feel caught

in the middle and homesick for both.

"But the reason why I'm broken, the reason why I cry, is how

long must I wait to be with you?"

- FROM THE MERCYME SONG "HOMESICK"

"HOMESICK"

By November 2003, MercyMe was ready for a well-deserved rest. The popularity of "I Can Only Imagine" meant endless touring and a year that was busier than any we'd ever experienced.

I had the attitude that we were "off the clock," but God had other ideas. In early December, a pregnant friend that my wife and I had grown up with lost the twins she had been carrying for five months. Because she was so far along in her pregnancy, it was necessary to deliver the babies. It was a devastating loss, and when I was asked to sing "I Can Only Imagine" at the memorial service, I agreed.

The service was so moving for me that I sat down and wrote what would become the chorus for "Homesick." But I didn't want to belittle a very personal moment by putting it into four or five minutes of music and trying to make it rhyme, so I tucked away the scribbled fragment of a song.

Then the funerals continued. My bandmate Jim Bryson lost his father, and then other deaths in my small hometown followed. It seemed like every other day someone close to us was passing away. It was heartbreaking. In a period of less than six weeks, we lost eight people that were close to us.

The eighth was my twenty-year-old brother-in-law, Chris. Chris had a relationship with the Lord but in recent years he had been experiencing some difficulties. He hit rock bottom in the early hours of January 3, 2004 and paid us a visit. We talked for several hours and Chris left around 4 a.m., only after promising to meet later that day with a friend of mine who ran a local church's college group. But Chris never made it to that appointment.

On the way home, he fell asleep at the wheel, crashed his car, and was killed instantly.

Devastated, I pulled out the "Homesick" lyrics I had

photo by Mike Scheuchzer

written weeks earlier and finished the song in time for the band to sing it at Chris' funeral. Despite my grief, I was really glad for the amazing opportunity we had to share the gospel and talk to his friends.

And that was pretty much the end of the song. It wasn't meant to go anywhere else, so I wadded up the lyrics and threw them away. Unlike "Imagine," which was less of an "I miss my dad" song and more of a pondering of Heaven and what we'll find there, "Homesick" was really just for the situation, for me and my wife and her family. We were confused, angry, and broken. We understood in our minds that there are no goodbyes in Christ, but the waiting hurts in our hearts just the same.

That may be why my mother-in-law was so insistent that I share the song. She said, "I think it's a tragedy to write something like that, knowing how other people go through what we're going through, and for them not to hear it."

I wasn't sure how to respond to that. Then I recalled what Holly, the mother who lost her twins, had said following their deaths: "I wish my twins could have lived long enough to make a difference." Needless to say, I had a change of heart. It felt great to be able to tell Holly, "Because of what you went through, [this song] could reach millions of people. So don't ever say your twins didn't live long enough to make a difference."

photo by Bart Millard

I'll never forget November 24, 2004—the day my daughter, Gracie, was born. Exactly two weeks later, my three-year-old son, Sam, was diagnosed with diabetes. I helplessly passed the hours at Children's Hospital, and for three or four days I wept continuously. The doctors would try to put it into perspective, to gently point out how much worse it could be. But they just didn't get it. It's not that I couldn't see the silver lining. I just couldn't get to that silver lining fast enough. Despite the ache of our situation, I still believed in a future without tears, death, or sorrow.

"Why?"

When we're hurting, when life doesn't make sense, it's almost impossible not to ask. But is there any answer that would satisfy us?

Job couldn't resist questioning God, but the Creator's reply surely wasn't what he expected. God didn't exactly respond with an answer. Instead He offered a few questions of His own. I see this as a not-so-gentle reminder that we can't see the whole picture and we're not supposed to. If we could, we wouldn't need God. All we can do is continue to trust the One who can see the whole picture.

It's easy for me to think that after all I've been through, I deserve some sort of free pass or that I should be immune from further loss or hurt. However, when I start to think about what I deserve I think about the immense pain Jesus suffered on my behalf, and I realize that if I got what I deserved, it would be so much worse.

"I know God won't give me more than I can handle.

I just wish He didn't trust me so much."

- MOTHER TERESA

"Homesick" *by Bart Millard*

You're in a better place

I've heard a thousand times

And at least a thousand times I've rejoiced for you

But the reason why I'm broken

The reason why I cry

Is how long must I wait to be with you?

I close my eyes and I see your face

If home is where the heart is, then I'm out of place

Lord, won't you give me strength to make it through somehow?

I've never been more homesick than now

Help me Lord 'cause I don't understand your ways

The reason why I wonder if I'll ever know

But even if you showed me, the hurt would be the same

'Cause I'm still here so far away from home

I close my eyes and I see your face

If home is where the heart is, then I'm out of place

Lord, won't you give me strength to make it through somehow?

I've never been more homesick than now

In Christ, there are no goodbyes

And in Christ there is no end

So I'll hold on to Jesus with all that I have

To see you again

And I close my eyes and I see your face

If home is where the heart is, then I'm out of place

Lord, won't you give me the strength to make it through somehow?

I've never been more homesick than now

"And as He was getting in the boat, the man who had been demon-possessed was entreating Him that he might accompany Him. And He did not let him, but He said to him, 'Go home to your people and report to them what great things the Lord has done for you and how He had mercy on you.'"

- MARK 5:18-19

Epilogue

In 1 Corinthians 13:12 Paul tells us that "For now we see in a mirror dimly, but then face to face; now I know in part, but then I shall know fully just as I also have been fully known."

That may explain why sometimes it can feel like we're fumbling through this life with poor vision and broken eyeglasses. But you have to read the whole verse to really understand the beautiful promise that one day we will see everything clearly. The puzzle pieces will fit into place, the mystery will be solved, our questions will be answered. Our homesickness — my homesickness — will find an end.

For now, though, the journey isn't over. We continue on, relying on God's guidance to point the way until we reach our final destination and can at last hear Him say, "Welcome home."

BART MILLARD is the lead singer of the Dove Award-winning band MercyMe. Their debut disc, *Almost There,* has been certified double-platinum, due in part to the huge success of their touching hit single, "I Can Only Imagine." Their most recent release, *Undone,* features the #1 hit song, "Homesick." Also look for a solo hymns recording from Millard in Summer 2005.

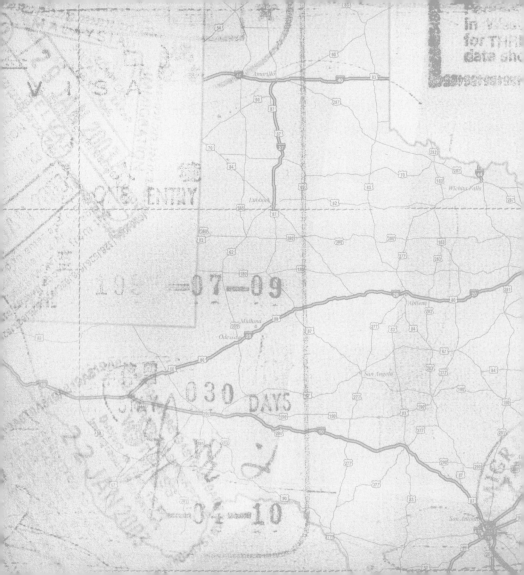